THE SIMPLE GUIDE TO
GERMANY
CUSTOMS AND ETIQUETTE

COVER ILLUSTRATION

Waitress demonstrating her beer-carrying
skills at the annual *Oktoberfest* in Munich

Photo Laurence Hughes. Courtesy Image Bank

ABOUT THE AUTHORS

WALTRAUD COLES has for many years taught the language,
culture and customs of Germany to beginners and honours students
alike at the University of Durham. UWE KOREIK has taught
German as a foreign language at a number of institutions, including
business schools and several universities in Europe. He is now
working at the University of Hanover.

*The authors extend their thanks to Oliver Coles and Dermot McElholm
for their suggestions and improvements*

ILLUSTRATED BY
IRENE SANDERSON

SIMPLE GUIDE TO

GERMANY

CUSTOMS & ETIQUETTE

WALTRAUD COLES
&
UWE KOREIK

GLOBAL BOOKS LTD

Simple Guides • Series 1
CUSTOMS & ETIQUETTE

The Simple Guide to
GERMANY
CUSTOMS & ETIQUETTE
by Waltraud Coles & Uwe Koreik

New edition 1995

First published 1995 by
Global Books Ltd
PO Box 219, Folkestone, Kent, England CT20 3LZ

Third Edition 1999

© Global Books Ltd 1999

ISBN 1–86034–031–8

British Library Cataloguing in Publication Data
A CIP catalogue entry for this book
is available from the British Library

Set in Futura 11 on 12 pt by Bookman, Hayes, Middlesex
Printed and bound in Malta by Interprint Ltd.

Contents

Foreword

King Ludwig II's Neuschwanstein castle, Bavaria

On the surface, things have hardly changed in the three years since the last Foreword was written. The process of modernizing the former East Germany is still continuing. In particular, the larger cities like Leipzig and Dresden, or even Jena in places, have a stylish post-modern look with old city-centre buildings being renovated in a truly impressive manner or even being rebuilt like the Frauenkirche in Dresden.

An extraordinary amount of construction work will continue to be done in the East for many years to come. Even on the outskirts of the cities, the often ugly Plattenbauten (buildings made from prefabricated blocks) need a 'face-lift' and thoroughly renovating, if not pulled down.

Anyone who is honest has to admit that a few years after unification there are indeed in the East some 'flourishing regions', just as the former Chancellor Helmut Kohl had promised the East Germans. However, many people, not only from the East, have had understandable difficulties accepting that Kohl's promise had at least been partly fulfilled because it seemed to conflict with the extremely high unemployment figures in many parts of the former East Germany.

One definite change that has affected the country has certainly been the move of the seat of government from the small and relatively quiet city of Bonn to the new capital, Berlin, much further to the east. The 'Berlin republic' is a slogan being used to indicate that a different era will be ushered in with the new millennium, when Germany will be governed once again from Berlin.

WALTRAUD COLES & UWE KOREIK
November 1998

1

Introducing Germany

'. . .Germans often identify themselves more with regions'

As everyone knows, as a result of the Second World War, Germany was divided into two countries. The division took place in 1949 when the two new German states were founded. Over the next four decades they developed in two completely different ways.

West Germany, exposed to and responsive to the cultural influences of the Western allies, especially the United States and Britain, set about building up its market economy and became increasingly prosperous. 'Achievement' became the key word both for the individual and the

MAP OF REUNITED GERMANY

community as a whole, and expectations grew rapidly with regard to both personal prosperity and social welfare. West Germans also became noted for their assertiveness and even personal relationships are, to some extent, subject to this attitude. At the same time, a strong sense of democracy developed with great emphasis being put on the individual's rights and duties within a democratic society.

In East Germany, under the political influence of the USSR and with an economy much less strong than its West German counterpart, the emphasis was on communal achievement. With all sorts of commodities every now and then in short supply a support network of friends and relatives made all the difference in coping. Thus, traditional values, such as those associated with family loyalty and friendship, were held in high regard. Some East Germans feared that after unification these positive aspects of their society could be undermined by what they regarded as the ruthlessness of Western society.

To some extent, developments since unification have confirmed these fears. With all commodities now freely available on the open market, the old network of friends and relatives is no longer required for former practical reasons. Thus, having lost its original importance, such relationships are no longer as close as they used to be. Copying Western attitudes, great emphasis is now put on an individual's success and achievement.

The 'new' Germany of the 1990s (and for that matter the new millennium) has never existed in its present form before. The frequently-used term 'reunification' is therefore somewhat misleading. The 'new' Germany, in fact, comprises the areas of Germany which, after the Second World War, were under the occupation of the Soviet Union and the Western Allies. The former easternmost areas (e.g. East Prussia and Silesia) were absorbed by Poland and Russia as a result of Germany having started the war.

Germany now has about 80 million inhabitants, made up of about 61 million from the former West Germany and 17 million from the former East Germany, as well as people who moved to Germany after unification, many of them from East European countries. More than 6.5 million people living in Germany today are foreigners. Thus, Germany has, after Russia, the biggest population in Europe. After Belgium and the Netherlands, Germany is the most densely-populated country in Europe. Roughly a third of the population lives in urban areas. With a total area of 357,529 km^2 or 138,043 square miles, Germany is smaller than both France and Spain.

Top Tip: Regional Identities

For historical reasons, Germans quite often identify themselves more with regions than with Germany as a whole. Many Bavarians, for example, would put Bavaria first – just as you might expect Scotsmen/ Texans to put Scotland/Texas before Britain/USA as a whole. Since unification, however, the idea of a national identity is being discussed frequently in the press.

FOCUS ON POST-UNIFICATION GERMANY

The pictures, broadcast all over the world, of Germans jubilantly breaking down the Berlin Wall on 9 November 1989, rejoicing in their new-found freedom, will not easily be forgotten. The official unification one year later was celebrated in an equally exuberant way. But once the euphoria had died down, disillusionment quickly set in. It became clear that unification would result in enormous costs to the country.

Unemployment rose steeply, especially in the East, where outdated factories were no longer competitive, and many were bought up by Western companies. In addition, people in the East were disappointed when they realized that uni-fication did not automatically mean improved living conditions and they began to see themselves again as 'second-class' citizens. As a result, they had to make enormous adjustments, not just in abstract terms, such as having to get used to living in a completely different society, but also in practical, daily life. Every single form they had to fill in had changed, completely different rules and regulations now applied to all spheres of public life. From the law on unemployment to the housing laws, from insurance policies to rental agreements, everything was suddenly very different indeed.

In the former West Germany the majority of people were hardly aware of any changes as a result of unification. Many of them, however, resented the increases in taxes that were required to pay for the costs of unification. Some people from the West, in fact, made a quick profit out of the East Germans, at first still largely ignorant of all the new regulations and options. This led to the cliché of the arrogant, profit-orientated, know-all *Wessi* (West German) and the naïve, slow, does-not-know-how-to-work-hard *Ossi* (East German). Thus, mutual mistrust developed and it will take many years before a more neutral relationship evolves, especially as far as the middle-aged and older generation are concerned.

The 'new' Germany also has a new capital: Berlin. Moving the seat of government from Bonn to Berlin was a controversial decision and was passed by the German parliament only with a very small majority. The move is going to be very expensive since a large number of new official buildings etc. have to be built. This process will, it is said, be completed by the year 2000. Until then Bonn remains the seat of government, although Berlin already is the official capital.

Berlin

THE *LÄNDER*

Germany is organized in federal states (the so-called *Länder*). The old ones in the former West Germany are **Bayern** (Bavaria) and **Baden-Württemberg** in the south, the small **Saarland** and **Rheinland-Pfalz** (Rhineland-Palatinate) in the southwest, **Hessen** (Hesse) and **Nordrhein-Westfalen** (North-Rhine-Westphalia) in the middle and the city states **Bremen** and **Hamburg** as well as **Niedersachsen** (Lower Saxony) and **Schleswig-Holstein** in the north.

In the former East Germany we find the 'new' *Länder*: **Mecklenburg-Vorpommern** in the north, **Brandenburg** in the centre and east, with a unified

Berlin in its middle, **Sachsen-Anhalt** in the west, **Thüringen** (Thuringia) in the southwest and **Sachsen** (Saxony) in the southeast.

The question whether some of the smaller *Länder* (e.g. the **Saarland**, or the city state **Bremen**) ought to be merged with one of the bigger *Länder* is frequently discussed. The *Länder* have autonomy in some matters. The most important of these is education.

HOLIDAYS

Top Tip: Rotating Holidays!

In an attempt to avoid traffic jams on motorways at the beginning and end of the school holidays, the summer holidays in the various *Länder* follow a rota system. The holiday period extends from mid-June to mid-September. Within this period holidays in each of the *Länder* last for six to seven weeks, each starting the holiday at a different time.

Like school holidays, public holidays vary in the *Länder*. Most public holidays were originally religious ones and whether or not they are still observed as holidays depends on whether the area is traditionally Catholic (mainly the south) or Protestant (mainly the north). Bavaria, for example, has 14 public holidays each year, whereas Hamburg only has 10.

Carnival time

Public holidays observed in all *Länder*:

New Year (1 January)
Good Friday
Easter Monday
May Day (1 May)
Ascension
Day of German Unity (3 October)
Christmas Day (25 December)
2nd Christmas Day (26 December)

In some areas of southern Germany and around Aachen, Mainz, Düsseldorf and Cologne in particular where carnival is celebrated, the Monday preceding Ash Wednesday is a quasi-public holiday. This day is the highlight of the carnival period when colourful processions take place and even those who might be described as 'serious Germans' can be seen to enjoy themselves and have fun in public!

'The direct approach is adopted in a wide range of situations'

THE GERMAN 'DIRECT' APPROACH

In many ways, Germans are very straightforward or 'matter-of-fact' as regards their attitude to personal relationships and social intercourse. Behaviour which might be regarded as bad manners in many other societies is considered to be 'natural' behaviour – and 'natural' for Germans equals 'honest'/'not false'. For example, two people whispering in the company of others is simply interpreted as two people discussing something which does not affect or concern the other people present, rather than as excluding those present. A person bumping into you by mistake may not necessarily apologize since, after all, Germans might say, it had not been done deliberately.

Top Tip: Germans Speak Their Mind!

Germans tend to be quite direct and they more or less say what they think. They usually come straight to the point without much polite small talk. This may appear rude to some foreigners, but it is certainly not intended to be. This direct approach is adopted in a wide range of situations, from complaining about bad service to flirting.

Many Germans tend to speak with a fairly loud voice. This, combined with the distinctive German intonation, might be interpreted as a sign of aggression. The two Germans you thought were quarrelling with one another are probably exchanging pleasantries!

For most Germans, especially those of the postwar generation, there are no real taboo topics of conversation. In some circles, however, such topics as religion or sex may be regarded as sensitive ones and some Germans still prefer not to talk specifically about the Third Reich and the last war. Others, on the other hand, welcome the opportunity to talk about these issues. Leave the initiative to them. Small-talk topics may include the state of one's health, some items in the news, sport and, perhaps, the weather.

Top Tip: Germans Do Have A Sense of Humour!

Contrary to the common stereotype, Germans do have a sense of humour! However, it is a different sense of humour and a joke which might get you a laugh at home might be seen as not funny at all. Black humour is often not recognized for what it is and rarely appreciated.

Another cliché, that of the *serious* German, is definitely true. Germans tend to be rather more serious about most things than people from many other countries. A remark which you had intended to be a lighthearted one and of no great importance, may be taken seriously by your German listener. As a result, you may be asked to elaborate on it, explain it . . .

THE GREEN MOVEMENT

One issue Germans are taking very seriously indeed these days is the question of the environment. The Green movement in Germany (see Ch.2) managed to raise public awareness of environmental concerns long before other nations became aware of the severity of the situation. Environmentally-friendly products are on sale everywhere and recycling is done systematically.

There are special containers for collecting paper, batteries, cans, and, quite literally, a bottle bank round every corner. However, it will take considerable time and resources to reverse the extensive damage done in the east to the environment during the period under the Communist regime.

'A sense of pride in one's environment'

The fact that German towns and cities always appear spotless (or, at least, very clean – usually, but not always!) to foreign visitors, however, has more to do with the German attitude towards tidiness than with environmental issues. The sense of pride in one's environment, the wish to keep everything tidy and in order seems to be one of the main characteristics of the German mind. Dropping litter in the middle of the street, for example, would be seen as a deliberate, offensive act, rather than merely a careless one.

2

The 'New Germans'

Semper's Opera House, Dresden

During the first decades of the twentieth century, German science and media made much of the issue of German character, which led to the feeling of supremacy on the part of the so-called Germanic or Aryan race. The Second World War and the Holocaust were the notorious results of this way of thinking. Since then many Germans have had problems with their nationality. Nearly a whole generation felt ashamed of what the older generation had been responsible for and did not feel proud to be German at all. They would prefer to regard themselves as Europeans.

Germany's early signal that it wished to generate a momentum towards a unified Europe must be seen as a consequence of the nation's feeling of guilt. The search for 'German identity' has been a major German preoccupation since the two German states were founded in 1949, and it has continued since their official unification on 3 October 1990. The problem many Germans had in identifying with their own nation was obvious, for example, when it came to national symbols. Compared to other nations, the Germans – especially the West Germans – were very reluctant to wave their national flag even on special occasions. This changed when the wall came down and the change could be clearly registered when the West German team won the soccer World Cup in 1990.

Despite the fact that some right-wing nationalist groups attract attention now and then, it seems as if the Germans are on their way to adopting a more relaxed attitude towards their nation and their role in Europe and the world.

Though the Germans have become quite inter-national in many ways you can nevertheless still observe certain differences in attitudes and behaviour – or to put it in more modern terms – different mentalities. The vast majority of Germans, for instance, still regard punctuality as a very important value. This is not only true for the old generation. On the other hand, many old hackneyed cliches do not really apply any more. Certainly the odd beer-drinking German can still be spotted and he might even wear short lederhosen at the Oktoberfest in Munich every year. But he has become a rare species and would only attract laughter in other parts of Germany.

AUTHORITY & THE ENVIRONMENT

The legendary German deference to authority – or subservience might be a better word for the behaviour of many Germans earlier in the century – is largely a thing of the past. Think of the so-called student revolution of 1968, where the stagnant conservatism of the Adenauer and post-Adenauer era (Chancellor of West Germany from 1949 to 1963) was overwhelmed by the protests of a generation of dissatisfied youth rebelling against the war in Vietnam and antiquated hierarchies in universities and in society in general. This was also the first generation of young people to question their parents' role during the Nazi era. Or think of the revolution that took place in East Germany, where hundreds of thousands of East Germans took to the streets and ousted their Communist masters.

Germany, in fact, used to be a very clean and tidy country, and elsewhere we note that German towns and cities appear spotless or at least very clean to foreigners. Nevertheless, a smaller town, let us say, in the country in southern Germany, is certainly quite different from the area around railway stations in large cities. Consider this story: a German and an American were walking through the streets of a medium-sized city where there was a lot of litter. The German pointed out the untidy state of the streets to the American and remarked sadly that Germany always used to be a clean country. The American replied that this must have been the Germany of his grandparents' generation.

Germans in a small village in, for example, Bavaria or Baden-Württemberg, can be very different from Germans living in a major northern city such as Hamburg or in a working-class town like Eisenhüttenstadt, close to the Polish border, which was planned along socialist lines. In many southern villages and towns there is still a *Kehrwoche* (keep-tidy week), which means that all the residents of a street have to take turns keeping their part of the street tidy. This would be unthinkable in other parts of the country. On the other hand you still find the old collective mentality in some parts of the former East Germany.

ATTITUDE TO CHANGE

Even a decade after unification many Germans have difficulties in accepting the change. Many West Germans have hardly been to the East after all this time and only a few are in contact with people from the former German Democratic Republic. On the other hand, many East Germans still have problems accepting the fact that this hard-won freedom also involves a loss of security and convenience. For example, everybody was guaranteed a job on the former socialist East Germany, and all the children were cared for in nursery schools. Both have changed significantly. Many kindergartens have had to be closed down for financial reasons or because the number of births have dropped dramatically.

Despite all the efforts of politicians unemployment has risen disproportionately in the East compared to the West. The winter of 1997/98 saw the highest unemployment figures in Germany since the 1930s' economic crisis of the Weimar Republic when Hitler came to power, and since the early post-war period when millions of people fled to the western part of Germany. Unemployment in the late nineties has become an immense problem, especially in the East where up to one in four of the working population is unemployed. This has led to disappointment, nostalgia and – particularly among younger people – to a protest in regional elections where they voted for extreme right-wing parties.

Nevertheless, the general election in autumn 1998 illustrated the normality of German democracy despite economic problems: after sixteen years in power the Chancellor, Helmut Kohl, was voted out of office by an astonishing majority who preferred Gerhard Schröder, the new candidate of the Social Democratic Party. He supposedly resembled Britain's Tony Blair in his electoral strategies and propagated a new political centreground. The Social Democrats, who regained their old strength, formed a coalition government together with the Green Party.

This was the first time in German post-war democracy that the whole government was forced into opposition by an election. Up to that point a new government has always been established by a change of coalition. The Greens are a child of the 1968 student riots referred to earlier, and they stand for pro-environment policies, an end to nuclear power, gender equality and a more just society generally.

The Greens' election success is a sign of the radical change – indeed upheaval – that has taken place in German society. And yet this is not even seen as an upheaval, nor has there been any real protest at the Greens being in government for the first time, something which would have been unthinkable even a few years ago. This indeed is the most important conclusion we can draw from our observations of German society, that the Germans have learnt to be rather more tolerant and flexible.

3

Festivals, Customs & Traditions

A Christmas branch and candle

CHRISTMAS

Christmas is the most important festival in the German calendar. It is, however, not on 25 December but on Christmas Eve that the main celebration takes place. Shops and offices close at midday and then everyone rushes home to prepare for the festivities.

Traditionally, a light meal is shared during late afternoon or early evening and then the family members gather in the living-room, specially decorated with branches from fir trees and candles, to sing or listen to carols and exchange presents. In religious households this may be preceded by the reading of appropriate passages from the Bible. Children usually find their presents under the Christmas tree. If they live in the north of Germany the *Weihnachtsmann*, a Father Christmas-type figure, is said to have brought the presents, whilst in the south it is an angel-like figure, the *Christkind*, which literally means 'Christ Child'. In Catholic areas, after the present-giving, people (even if they are not regular church-goers) traditionally attend midnight mass in the local church.

The traditional German Christmas tree, a fir tree, is decorated with special Christmas orna-ments. These ornaments vary greatly from area to area and family to family. You might see silver- or gold-coloured ones, others are made of glass; there are also colourful toy-like wooden miniatures, depicting animals, angels and other Christmas themes, and in some areas you find delicate stars and other intricate shapes made of straw. Tradi-tionally, the straw was flattened with a hot iron until various shades of brown were achieved and then these strips of straw were shaped into festive patterns.

Nowadays, you can, of course, buy these decorations ready-made, but during the pre-Christmas period parents, children and young people at home, in schools, kindergartens, and some youth clubs still make them themselves. Small candles in special clip-on holders are also used to decorate the tree. For safety reasons, however, these have mostly been replaced by electric candles.

The Christmas Eve celebration is essentially a family affair. Friends and colleagues exchange presents earlier in the day or on the day before or after. It would be considered most unusual, even rude, to disturb a family during these special hours. On the other hand, 25 December is increasingly considered to be simply a public holiday. Although members of the wider family circle, such as aunts and uncles may arrive for a visit, it is not considered unusual for young people to go off to visit friends or to go skiing.

Top Tip: Look Out For Christmas Markets!

Special Christmas markets are held each year in many German towns and cities where, amongst other things, traditional Christmas decorations and food can be bought. Do not be surprised or disappointed, though, if the packaging for the ornament you bought tells you that it was made in China! One of the most famous markets is the *Christkindlesmarkt* in Nuremberg. The tradition there goes back hundreds of years, and thousands of tourists come from all over the world to visit it.

Christmas cake (*Stollen*) and traditional Christmas biscuits, often spicy or with chocolate, nuts or marzipan, and the famous gingerbread (*Lebkuchen*) are sold everywhere. Hot *Glühwein* (mulled wine) which can be bought at many stalls is the traditional drink to go with these special cakes and biscuits. The markets would not be complete without several stalls also selling fried sausages. Choirs sing and (brass) bands play Christmas carols and other traditional music.

Four weeks before Christmas, children are given a so-called *Adventskalender* (Advent Calendar). This has a little 'door' for each day up to Christmas. Hidden behind each door is a picture or even a bit of chocolate. People have special wreaths with four candles, one to be lit on each Sunday before Christmas. On 6 December in many areas, a man dressed up as St Nicholas visits children in schools and nurseries or even at home. The children recite poems or sing a song and if they have been good throughout the year, they are given sweets, nuts, oranges and apples. Children who did not behave well are dealt with by St Nicholas' helper. He carries a birch rod and a sack to carry off naughty children! Fortunately, his services are never really called upon!

NEW YEAR

The coming of the New Year (1 January) is celebrated in style, with noisy bangers and fireworks everywhere late on New Year's Eve. At the stroke of midnight, church bells ring in the New Year. There are parties everywhere and at some, people traditionally drop hot lead into a bowl of water, and from the resulting strange shapes they tell their fortunes – much to the amusement of everyone present! Sometimes symbols of good luck are exchanged, such as little pigs, chimney-sweeps, four-leaf clover, horseshoes and lady-birds, usually made of marzipan or chocolate.

Epiphany: 'three Wise Men'

At *Heilige Dreikönige* (Epiphany, 6 January) in Catholic areas three children, or even teen-age boys or young men, dress up as the Three Wise Men and go from house to house. They recite blessings and also collect money for charity and are rewarded for their efforts with sweets. You may notice above the inside of the main entrance doors the letters C+M+B (supposedly the initials of the Three Wise Men) and the year written with chalk by the three visitors. This is left all year until it is replaced with the new inscription the following year. Originally organized by the local church, in recent years enterprising youngsters have recog-nized this as an easy way to get sweets or money and so you may encounter more than one group of Wise Men!

FEBRUARY CARNIVALS

In February major carnivals are held in many parts of Germany. These are occasions for people to dress up in fancy dress and wear masks. The patterns for some of these masks and costumes are centuries old and vary greatly from area to area. Some of the oldest ones, such as witches or monsters, are quite startlingly grotesque. There are many carnival societies, some of them with very long traditions. The start date for the preparation of the floats for the processions is on the 11th day of the 11th month at 11 minutes past 11 o'clock. Many cities, towns and villages have a carnival prince and princess. They are also the central focus of many carnival processions, which are usually held on the Sunday or Monday before Ash Wednesday.

In some cities such as Cologne these processions are quite spectacular and last for hours. Streamers and sweets are thrown from the floats at the spectators lining the streets. There are parties everywhere, in offices, schools and at home, and even in the most sober of council offices and departments you may be served by people in fancy dress.

Whilst Germans normally address strangers with a polite form of address (*Sie*) the familiar form (*du*) is used by many people in some areas during carnival time. This, of course, reverts to the polite form the moment carnival is over and the 'serious' German takes over again.

EASTER

Easter, too, has its own customs. Traditionally, the whole family joins in to dye or paint colourful patterns onto hard-boiled eggs. On Easter Sunday children then hunt for these eggs in the garden, supposedly left there by the *Osterhase* (Easter bunny). Family members give each other chocolate eggs or bunnies and other sweets. Many people bring in bare branches from the garden and dress them with cheerful Easter decorations. In some areas, especially in the south, the fountain in the market-place or in front of the church is elaborately, and often beautifully, decorated with Easter flowers or even colourful blown eggs.

In rural areas there are many customs and traditions associated with saints' days. On St Martin's Day in November, for example, children carry paper lanterns through the streets. In Catholic areas processions are held on Corpus Christi Day. Traditionally, masses of flower petals were arranged in intricate patterns like carpets on the

ground in front of specially erected outdoor altars at the side of the streets through which the procession passes.

There are many non-religious customs, again with great regional variations. You may, for example, see what looks like a small Christmas tree decorated with colourful ribbons fixed on top of the yet untiled roof beams of a house that is being built. This is to celebrate the completion of the shell of the house and all craftsmen and workers employed in the building of the house attend this special celebration. Traditionally, a barrel of beer and all other refreshments are, of course, paid for by the owner.

ANNUAL FAIRS

Most cities, towns and villages have their annual fairs. In rural areas this is often held on the day of the anniversary of the consecration of the church. Thus, there often is a church service and a procession in the morning and a funfair in the afternoon. For many people, heavy drinking is part of the programme on this day and beer tents are put up specially to facilitate this. To keep up with the demand, waitresses have to carry several huge beer mugs at the same time, often even without using a tray. Waitresses at the famous Munich *Oktoberfest*, visited by many thousands of tourists each year, are especially renowned for this balancing act (see front cover).

In Catholic areas people used to celebrate their so-called name day; that is, the day of the saint one shares one's name with. This custom, however, has now been almost completely replaced by the celebration of one's birthday. Not only children but adults, too, celebrate their birthdays in style. In the work-place the person having a birthday usually arranges and pays for a (small) celebratory party. A person who is not prepared to do this is considered to be a real miser and might have to put up with a lot of teasing throughout the following year.

On their first day at primary school, children are given a large colourful, sometimes glossy, cardboard cone filled with all sorts of sweets, pens, toys, books etc. to sweeten their entry into school. When buying these so-called *Schultüten* parents and relatives often vie with each other to acquire the biggest and most impressive ones and sometimes these are almost as big as the child him/herself.

Schultüten

WEDDING TRADITIONS

In Germany, to be legally married, a couple has to attend the appropriate registry office ceremony. They have the option to have a church wedding in addition to this. In many areas, the night before the wedding the couple, together with friends and relatives, celebrate noisily at a so-called *Polterabend*. Traditionally, the highlight of this party is the smashing of crockery, collected for months or specially purchased for this very purpose.

Often practical jokes are played on the couple by their friends on the actual wedding day. High-jacking the bride on the morning of the wedding is just one of the many tricks the bridegroom's friends might get up to. Note that married people wear their wedding rings on the ring finger of their right hand. Wearing the ring on the left indicates that a couple is engaged.

NEW TRADITIONS

Traditions which have been established in recent years include the so-called *Familientreffen*. This is a get-together of the wider family circle, usually once a year. With families getting smaller and smaller, and with increasing mobility, living further and further away from one another, these meetings with cousins, aunts and uncles, grandparents and grandchildren have become very important to many people, since they are the only opportunity to get to know their relatives. Like many other celebrations in Germany, these meetings are usually centred around shared meals.

Top Tip: Germany's Keep-fit Preoccupation

Germans like to show that they are keeping fit. Wherever you go there are so-called *Trimm-Dich-Pfade*. These are a sort of keep-fit trail, in local parks and woods, where signs tell you when to do your press-ups and other exercises. Less energetic Germans stick to their regular Sunday afternoon walk, the *Sonntagsspaziergang*, a tradition which is religiously observed by some people.

In cities, with a large proportion of the population living in flats, parks and public gardens play a very important role for many people. Especially during summer weekends these places teem with life. All sorts of activities take place: various games are played, from football to open-air chess (where almost man-sized figures are moved around by the players), and there may also be open-air theatre.

Note, however, that in some parks you may not be permitted to walk on some of the lawns. The sign *Betreten verboten* tells you if you are not allowed to walk on the grass. There are also many outdoor swimming pools where, during the usually hot summer months, many children spend most of their free time. Germans also love barbecues. For the many flat-dwellers without balconies or gardens, special *Grillplätze* are provided in public parks and woods.

4

Meeting People

'. . .everybody is entitled to be treated with respect'

It is customary to shake hands both at the beginning of a meeting with someone and when saying goodbye. There is not really a clear rule about who offers his/her hand first, though in general the host or more senior person takes the initiative. If entering a room where several people are present it is usual to shake hands with every person there. Not responding to an outstretched hand or refusing to shake hands may be regarded at best as bad manners and at worst a deliberate snub. However, especially amongst younger people, and in more internationally-orientated circles, this attitude is slowly changing.

Top Tip: Always Say Hello

When entering a shop, office or even railway compartment it is customary to greet people and to say goodbye when leaving. The simplest and most useful greeting is *Guten Tag* (literally: Good Day=Good morning/afternoon, Hello). The German for 'goodbye' is *Auf Wiedersehen*.

TWO FORMS OF ADDRESS

In German there are two forms of address, that is to say two different words for 'you'. One is *du*, which is used for family members, close friends, children and sometimes members of the same club; the other is *Sie*, which is used for everybody else. The use of first names is virtually restricted to those for whom *du* is used. A relationship needs to develop into a fairly close one before it is decided to adopt the familiar *du* form and to use first names. Even colleagues who have been sitting in the same office for 20 years may still use the formal form and address each other by their surname and title, i.e. *Herr* . . . for a man or *Frau* . . . for a woman, whatever their age or marital status. If someone is introduced who has an academic title this may be added too, e.g. *Herr Dr* . . . *Frau Professor Dr* . . . Though the academic him/herself, out of a certain understatement, may not always use these titles.

On the whole, everybody, whatever their rank or position in life, is regarded as being entitled to be treated with respect and that includes being addressed by their title and surname, unless a mutual agreement alters this.

Top Tip: Don't Be Familiar!

If you address someone straight away by their first name this may be regarded as rude and presumptuous. Note, however, that in certain circles, for example amongst students and in some German subsidiaries of international companies, the use of first names is common. If in doubt about which form is appropriate keep to *Sie* and the surname.

ATTITUDE TO FOREIGNERS

Germans tend to be friendly and hospitable towards foreign visitors, at least when they clearly are tourists or on business. Foreign workers from Eastern or Southern Europe or from non-European countries, however, are often at the receiving end of xenophobic attitudes. At the beginning of the 1990s violent attacks on foreigners were committed by young people, driven by a sense of purposelessness and looking for a scapegoat for problems such as unemployment and a loss of security. These attacks shocked the majority of Germans to such an extent that they took to the streets in their hundreds of thousands, demonstrating against racism and violence against foreigners.

'. . .7.00 o'clock sharp'

INVITATIONS & HOME LIFE

Since English is a compulsory subject in German schools most Germans speak at least some English and many are keen to practise it. Germans love to talk at length about politics, current affairs, philosophy – you name it – and often discussions may go on until very late indeed. Leaving early (and that may mean as late as 11.00 pm!) may be regarded as a sign that you did not enjoy yourself. If hosts or other guests are yawning, this has to be interpreted as a sign of genuine tiredness rather than as dropping hints.

Large German families are rare. Families with only one or two children predominate and a large number of couples opt for not having any children. With the German population decreasing, there are frequent calls for a change in the tax system which would encourage people to start or add to their families. So far, none of these initiatives has been successful.

PRESENT-GIVING

When you are invited to someone's house, be it for drinks, afternoon coffee or an evening meal, it is the custom to take flowers rather than, for example, a bottle of wine. How much you pay for the bouquet depends on the occasion. An invitation for dinner, especially if you do not know your hosts very well yet, or if it is a social invitation in a business context, calls for a fairly substantial bouquet or, alternatively, an arrangement of exotic flowers. If you are not sure what might suit a particular occasion consult the florist. Florists' shops are a common feature in all German towns and cities and are invariably found in large railway stations and at airports; flowers are even sold from vending machines!

The correct form of presenting flowers is to unwrap them in the presence of your hostess. The wrapping paper may then be left on a hall table or, as some experts advise, in the umbrella stand! Since unwrapping the bouquet and disposing of the paper may prove a rather difficult operation for some people, it may be wiser to ask for the flowers to be wrapped in cellophane which then leaves the task of unwrapping them to the hostess!

In recent years, there seems to have been a slight trend away from bringing flowers, not least for practical reasons. The custom of bringing flowers goes back to times when there were servants ready to assist with receiving them. These days, your hostess, preoccupied as she will be with food preparation as well as welcoming guests, may appreciate an alternative gift. If you opt for not bringing flowers make sure you choose something unusual and special instead.

'. . .it is the custom to take flowers'

If you get invited to a meal in somebody's home make sure you arrive at the stated time. If the invitation is for 7.00 o'clock in the evening, for example, you are expected at 7.00 o'clock sharp and your hosts may have planned the cooking time accordingly.

The exchange of gifts is a well-established feature of social intercourse in Germany. Living in an affluent society Germans give presents not only at traditional times like Christmas and birthdays but also on many other occasions and for many reasons. Often they may simply be a small token of continuing friendship. For example, in shops and cafés you can purchase miniature boxes containing one chocolate with gift cards attached wishing the recipient of the gift a 'nice day' or 'good night'.

Home-made gifts are especially popular. If you are visiting from abroad a gift characteristic of your home country will, of course, be greatly appreciated. Do not forget also to bring small gifts for the children of the family you are visiting.

It is the custom to wrap gifts and many Germans make an art form out of wrapping up presents. Women's magazines frequently contain articles on how to wrap up gifts. Most shops and department stores (except food shops like supermarkets) will gift-wrap items you have bought without extra charge. However, the Green movement has had its impact and many people tend to buy recycled wrapping paper now. Some very environmentally-conscious people prefer not to wrap gifts at all or, indeed, make a point by wrapping up their presents in old newspaper and string!

Some shops hand out small gifts to their customers to thank them for their custom. Pharmacies, for example, may include a complimentary packet of paper handkerchiefs. At Christmas/New Year many shops give special calendars or diaries to their regular customers.

5

The German Home

'. . .flats rather than houses'

The majority of Germans live in flats rather than houses. Property ownership, however, is on the increase, even in the east of the country, where until 1989 it was rare for people to own their own homes. Most Germans, however, continue to rent their flats and houses. Since less money is spent on the purchase of a home a larger proportion of people's income is available for the purchase of furnishings, kitchen equipment etc., and it goes without saying that most German homes are very well appointed. Germans also tend to be extremely house-proud and thus ensuring that their homes are kept immaculately clean and tidy. Home-owners are obliged by law to keep the pavements outside their houses swept (and, in winter, free of snow). In apartment blocks there is usually a rota for these duties.

Top Tip: Table Culture

Germans love to sit around tables and many forms of entertainment are centred round one.

Not all homes have a separate dining-room but use instead a corner of the sitting-room. In smaller flats there is usually a dining corner in the kitchen.

In the bathroom you may see a pile of very small towels – about the size of face flannels. These are guest handtowels. If there is no container obviously intended for the used towel leave it to dry at the side of the bath or on the radiator.

OVERNIGHT STAY

If you are staying overnight with a German family, check their breakfast arrangements. In many homes, especially at weekends, breakfast is taken by the whole family at the same time and you might be expected to join in. Since Germans tend to get up fairly early (6.30–7.00 am) this may mean a rather early start to the day.

In some southern areas of Germany pastry may be served for breakfast on Sundays, or indeed during the week if it is to honour a guest, instead of the traditional bread rolls, butter and jam. In recent years, due to the growing interest in healthy eating, what is served for breakfast varies greatly. There may be Muesli, cornflakes, cheese, slices of cold meat and sausage, or soft-boiled eggs, but never fried food.

MEALS

Lunch is traditionally the main cooked meal of the day. German children attend school in the morning only and are usually home for lunch. In families where both parents are working there may be a cooked evening meal instead of a cooked lunch.

The traditional German evening meal (served between 6.00 and 7.00 pm) invariably consists of various cold cooked meats, cheeses, fish etc. served with bread or rolls. Beer, cider, wine, mineral water or tea (often herbal teas) may be served with it. However, if guests are invited, it is more likely to be a cooked evening meal served at a later time, usually at, say, 7.30 or 8.00 pm.

If you are invited *Zum Kaffee* that means traditionally mid-afternoon coffee. If it is a formal invitation you may be faced with a formidable choice of cakes, gateaux and pastry. It may be a hard thing to do, but try to sample as many as you can manage; if you do not, your German hosts might assume you do not like any of them!

6

Eating & Drinking

'. . .why not try a German beer'

Germany has become a multicultural society, at least as far as eating and drinking is concerned. You will find foreign restaurants even in smaller towns and as a result of widespread foreign travel German home cooking has, in many families, become more international too. Greek and Italian restaurants are particularly popular, with increasing numbers of Chinese restaurants opening up.

For a quick and reasonably-priced meal you should look for a *Steh-Imbiß*(*stube*) or *Schnellimbiß* (kiosks where you eat standing up).

There you do not only get the inevitable *Pommes Frites*, or more colloquially *Fritten* (chips) and *Bratwurst* (fried sausage) but also a variety of salads or kebabs if run by a Greek or Turkish owner. In medium-sized and larger cities you will certainly find the main international fast-food chains plus some slightly more authentic chains like *Nordsee* (fish) and *Wienerwald* (chicken).

If you want to sample a typically regional dish go to a real German *Gasthof* or *Gasthaus* (inn). The type of meal you will get there varies greatly from region to region. In the north you may be served a fish dish, in the south some kind of meat with *Knödel* (dumplings).

GERMAN BEER

With your meal why not try a German beer. Do not opt for a *Pils* if you are in a hurry. Drawing it in the traditional way takes seven to eight minutes, and it is regarded as the real thing only if the head rises above the top of the glass. Every region has its speciality. In the region of Cologne you might like to sample a *Kölsch*, or an *Alt* if you are in Düsseldorf. In the east of Germany there are numerous excellent types of *Pils* on offer. In the south you ought to try a *Weizenbier*. In many regions beer is often accompanied by a glass of *Schnaps* (spirits).

When choosing wine remember the words *süß* and *lieblich* (sweet) and *trocken* (dry). A *Tafelwein* might accompany an everyday meal.

There is also *Qualitätswein* (officially tested quality wine) or a high-class *Qualitätswein mit Prädikat* like *Kabinett*, or a *Spätlese* if you prefer a sweeter wine.

PUB/RESTAURANT ETIQUETTE

Even if you are only buying drinks, you will be served at your table and you do not have to get or order them at the bar. It is usual for the waiter or waitress to mark the number of drinks you are having on your beer-mat and s/he will add them up when you ask for your bill.

Traditionally, the man enters the restaurant first in order to check if the place is suitable and to see if there is a free table that is acceptable. Usually, you are allowed to choose a table yourself. In some medium-priced and in high-class restaurants you will be shown to your table.

When starting a meal Germans usually say *Guten Appetit*. When drinking they say *Pros(i)t* or *Zum Wohl* (cheers or to your health). When Germans drink to your health you are supposed to drink as well.

Top Tip: How to Calculate the Tip!

As regards tipping, in pubs it is the custom to round up the total sum of your bill to the nearest respectable full figure. For example, if your bill comes to 36.90DM give the waiter/waitress 40.00DM and perhaps say *'Das stimmt so'*, (literally, it is correct like this, meaning, of course, the difference is for you) or simply *'Das ist okay'*. When the bill is brought to the table on a plate simply leave a tip of between 5% and 10%. However, you are not obliged to do so and should certainly not do so if you have reason to be dissatisfied.

7

Business Matters

'. . .the working day begins very early'

German companies pride themselves on their efficiency and reliability and they expect the same from their trade partners. Letting a company down on a delivery date or the quality of the product, or getting the specification wrong, will in most cases disqualify the offending party from receiving further orders.

Although a large number of German business people speak some English (some indeed have an excellent command of the language) making the effort to speak at least a little bit of German creates a very positive impression and is especially important if you want to sell something to a German company. In the latter case many German companies simply insist on speaking German. Also, make sure that the sales/information brochures you bring to a meeting are already translated into German.

Note that in the German business world only the written word is legally binding. A 'gentlemen's agreement' can only be seen as a first step in the negotiations and any written contracts and agreements need to be checked meticulously by both parties involved.

THE WORKING DAY

The working day begins very early. Factory workers usually start work at 6.00 am. Many offices open as early as 7.00 am. Since most companies operate flexi-time, office hours may extend over a long period from 7.00 o'clock in the morning to 5.00 or 6.00 o'clock in the evening. The rush-hour is usually between 7.00 and 8.00 o'clock in the morning and between 4.00 and 6.00 o'clock in the evening. On Fridays, however, it may start earlier, at around 2.00 pm. There is usually a short coffee break between 9.00 and 10.00 o'clock in the morning and a short afternoon break at around 3.00 pm. The lunch break (30 minutes to 1 hour) is normally taken between 11.30 am and 1.00 pm.

A ppointments at 8.00 o'clock in the morning are regarded as normal, even for meetings with senior and top management. And if the appointment is for 8.00 am you are expected to be there at 8.00 am sharp.

Top Tip: Be Punctual!

Unpunctuality is seen not so much as a sign of rudeness but as a lack of self-discipline and as an indicator of unreliability. Many company directors and senior managers pride themselves on the fact that they begin work at the same time as their workers.

D o not forget to shake hands when meeting someone both at the beginning of the meeting and before leaving. If you are introduced to several people in the room it is usual to shake hands with everyone present.

DRESS CODE

D ress carefully when visiting prospective clients or business contacts in German. The way one dresses is seen as an expression of one's attitudes and opinions. Creased trousers and a sports jacket (let alone dirty shoes!) may not be attributed to a long journey and living out of a suitcase but might be interpreted as being part of a different life-style, or even worse, as inefficiency and unreliability, not conducive to business. A well-cut suit is a must for most business meetings.

'Dress carefully when visiting prospective clients'

Modern Germany, as already reviewed else-where, is, on the whole, a very democratic society. Canteens, car parks and washrooms are often shared by workers and management alike. Everybody (and that really does mean everybody) is regarded as being entitled to be addressed by his/her full title and surname. (*Herr/Frau XYZ*). Very senior colleagues and directors are sometimes addressed by their full job title (e.g. *Herr General-direktor, Frau Chefingenieurin* etc). In large compa-nies with a more international approach the use of first names for colleagues at the same level is slowly becoming more acceptable. Even here, however, the formal way of addressing people may be used when attending official meetings.

BUSINESS & PLEASURE

Germans do not find it easy to mix business and private life and tend to entertain business clients mainly in hotels and restaurants. Only after several meetings, if one gets on well privately as well as in business, and, indeed, at top management level, if a big business deal is being negotiated, an invitation to a private home is extended, usually to an evening meal. Note, however, that if you want to sell something to a German company it is you who is expected to do the entertaining, and that means to extend an invitation to a restaurant and pay for meals etc.

Top Tip: Choosing Tokens of Appreciation

Many companies present the person dealing with a particular sale, or an especially helpful PA or secretary, with a small token of appreciation (complimentary diaries, calculators, pens, etc. incorporating the company's logo) at the end of a successful meeting. At Christmas, and sometimes even at Easter, presents such as calendars, books, etc. are presented to business clients and loyal customers.

8

Travelling in Germany

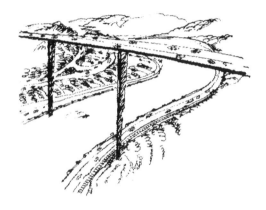

'A network of high-speed motorways'

In the former West Germany there is an extensive
and mostly excellently-maintained network of
high-speed motorways. Not even the strong
ecological movement has so far managed to
achieve a general speed limit. The majority of
German drivers would regard any speed restric-
tions as interfering with their personal rights.

So do take care. Stay on the far right-hand lane
until you yourself want to overtake and then
be careful not to underestimate the speed of

vehicles coming up behind. The flashing of head-lights on motorways must, more often than not, be interpreted as a threatening (illegal!) signal to 'get-out-of-the-way' rather than a polite sign that one driver wants to give another driver the right of way.

In the east some new motorways have already been built, some of the old ones are being modernized, and there are also new ones under construction or still in the planning phase. In the east, too, there is now officially no speed limit on motorways, but the still very mixed general state of their repair means that over long distances there is often a speed limit imposed. These frequent road works, as well as the general congestion due to rapidly increasing car ownership, mean, of course, that you have to allow more time when travelling in these parts of Germany.

ROAD SENSE

Where speed limits are in force, both in the east and in the west of Germany, frequent radar controls are carried out.

Long tailbacks must be expected at the beginning and end of the school holidays, despite the fact that the dates of school holidays in the different *Länder* are staggered throughout the summer in an attempt to avoid traffic chaos. In the vicinity of large cities, Stuttgart, Cologne and Munich in particular, traffic also builds up during the rush-hour, which may be as early as 7.00 am.

If there are no signs saying otherwise vehicles coming from the right at crossroads and junctions always have right of way.

In urban traffic watch out for cyclists. On the whole, they are regarded as road users with rights equal to motorists and they ride their bicycles with extraordinary confidence. There are cycle paths running alongside roads in most towns and cities. Turning right, thus crossing a cycle track, you have to give way to a cyclist even if you have overtaken him/her.

'. . .watch out for cyclists'

German drivers do not necessarily stop at zebra crossings. Before stopping make sure that the car behind you is not too close. On the other hand, car drivers are expected to give pedestrians the right of way when they are trying to cross the road in narrow side streets or exits.

B e careful when following a tram. If it stops to let passengers get on or off at a stop in the middle of the road you must wait behind the tram until all passengers have cleared the street.

I llegal parking, for example on a cycle track, or generally obstructing other vehicles, can lead to the car being towed away. The police will tell you how to get your car back and where to pay the hefty fine.

Top Tip: What To Do In An Accident

When an accident occurs every road user is obliged by law, first of all, to secure the scene of an accident by switching on flashing warning lights, then to display the warning triangle, which has to be carried in the car, and then to give first-aid if necessary. Take care if, as a driver from abroad, you have not been obliged to attend a first-aid course. If further injuries occur due to the injured person having been handled wrongly, you may be sued later by the person you gave first aid to or indeed by his/her relatives.

E ven with less serious accidents it is wise to call the police. In any case, make a note of the car registration number, name and address of the driver involved and possibly his/her motor insurance company. It is customary to exchange car documents (which German drivers have to carry with them) for copying and verifying these data. Where possible or necessary try to take the names and addresses of witnesses.

In former East Germany you may still find green arrows at traffic lights allowing one to turn right at junctions when the traffic lights show red. This is one of the very few things which were officially adopted in the west. It seems, however, that this good idea did not catch on there after all. Apart from these green arrows in the east and the very few installed in the west, you are only allowed to ignore the red light when the side turning clearly avoids the traffic lights altogether.

If you drink alcohol before driving bear in mind that you are only allowed 0.5 *Promille* (i.e. an alcohol level of 50 milligrams per 100 millilitres of blood). Note that some people may reach this level after only a single beer. Random breath tests are frequently carried out throughout Germany.

PUBLIC TRANSPORT

Germany has an extensive public transport network. There are hourly fast train connections between major cities, and even smaller cities and towns can boast a fairly frequent service. Note that if you use one of the numerous express trains for a distance of less than 50 km you have to pay a special supplement on the train. Special trains to trade fairs have first-class seats only. All stations are 'open stations', i.e. there are no platform barriers, tickets being checked on the train.

For longer journeys, free seat reservations are recommended. Tickets can be bought not only at stations but for the same price at specially licensed travel agents displaying the sign DB=*Deutsche Bundesbahn*. There is often less queuing there and staff will probably speak English. Look out for special discounts for travelling during certain times. By purchasing a so-called *Bahncard* (available both for individuals and families) the price of any ticket you buy is then halved. If you travel frequently a *Bahncard* may quickly pay for itself. In 'green' circles owning a *Bahncard* is a must.

A special service exists to transport your luggage directly from your home or hotel to the place where you will be staying at your destination. Details of this service are available from stations.

In rural areas extensive bus networks make even fairly remote areas accessible to public transport users. Many cities have good tram networks and several also offer an underground train service.

Note that in most cases you have to purchase your ticket before boarding the bus, tram or underground. There are ticket machines at most major stops. You may then have to cancel the ticket or sections of a multi-journey ticket by inserting it into a machine which stamps it, either before entering or on board the vehicle.

9

Out & About

'. . .a certain assertiveness is called for'

SHOPPING

Previously very rigid regulations governing SHOP OPENING HOURS are undergoing changes. At the time of going to press normal opening hours are:

On Thursdays shops usually do stay open until 8.00 pm or sometimes even 8.30 pm. On other days it can be very different. Many shops still close at the traditional time, which is 6.30 pm. On Saturdays many shops, in particular larger department stores and bigger supermarkets, stay open until 4.00 pm, but they are talking about extending Saturday opening hours as well. On Sundays more and more bakeries have opened in the morning to sell traditional bread rolls (and a wide variety of bread and pastry).

Many shops and supermarkets in rural areas and small shops in towns and cities are closed during the lunch period, sometimes for as long as two hours.

Some supermarkets, shops and kiosks in railway stations and airports may have different opening hours. Many petrol stations have small supermarket-like shops attached to them which are open 24 hours a day.

The fact that there are exceptions to the opening hours for some of these shops and the fact that the working hours for more and more people are becoming ever more flexible will, sooner or later, despite resistance from the trade unions, lead to a further relaxation in the rules about opening hours.

BANKS are open on Mondays–Fridays: 8.30 am–12.30 pm; 2.00–4.00 pm.
On Thursdays they open until 5.30 or 6.00 pm.
On the many public holidays all shops, banks and offices are closed.

Germany, on the whole, is still a fairly cash-orientated society and many shops do not yet accept credit cards. If they do so a sign at the entrance door indicates which ones are accepted. Most shops, however, take Euro-cheques.

Top Tip: The Queue ('Line-up') Has Arrived!

There is no tradition of forming queues ('line-ups'). But in recent years, in places such as banks, post offices and other public offices, queuing has been introduced, and even in other places the principle of 'first come, first served' usually applies.

GETTING SERVED

In smaller shops and in rural areas it is considered very rude to try to get served before the person who entered the shop before you. On the other hand, in large and crowded shops during busy periods it can be difficult at times to get served at all, since people push past one to get service. In these cases a certain assertiveness is called for! Shop assistants tend to be helpful and polite. Many of them will have undergone some thorough training and take a certain pride in their selling skills.

Most public buildings, council offices, etc. follow the same pattern of opening as shops, i.e. opening early and closing during the lunch period. Some will be closed in the afternoon.

When dealing with German officialdom be prepared for rigid rules and regulations. The amount of paperwork needed for some procedures is phenomenal. Trying to cut corners may prolong matters. Most officials are helpful and know their subject. But 'rules are rules' seems to be the slogan and attempts to get round the rules rather than comply with them are not tolerated. Anyhow, many civil servants have become more friendly and tolerant during the last few years.

TELECOMMUNICATIONS

Public telephones usually are in good working order. The telephone network has been privatized and now runs under the name Telekom. Telekom has invested in an ultra-modern telecommunications network now spanning the entire Federal Republic. You can phone abroad from phone boxes with the sign '*International*' or '*Ausland*'. Pictograms in the phone kiosks show you how to use the phone, which coins to use, etc. A large number of public phones can be operated by phone cards. You can buy phone cards in the post office, at kiosks and sometimes at hotel receptions. Some phone boxes, displaying a special sign, allow you to use credit cards. In some call boxes you can receive calls as well as making them. The dialling tones you hear on German phones may differ from the ones you are used to.

During the last few years a rapid change in the telephone system in Germany has been taking place. Several call-by-call service providers offer cheaper calls within Germany and other countries. For example Arcor with the number 01070 at the beginning of the number you want to dial, and TelDelFax with the code 01030 or Viatel (01079) are companies you might save money with. But be sure to get up-to-date information because things are changing quickly.

Looking up a number in a German telephone directory can be difficult because entries are organized in a way which often puzzles foreign visitors. The main reason for this is that German is an inflected language. Therefore '*Deutsche Lufthansa*' would be listed before '*Deutscher Hof*'. Entries which contain a letter with a so-called *Umlaut* (the two dots above a, o, u → ä, ö, ü) are listed alphabetically after the letter without an *Umlaut*. Telekom is currently looking into the way entries are listed. If you need a phone number within Germany you can phone one of the information service lines: e.g. 11833 for Telekom or 11880 and 11811 run by smaller companies. For international numbers dial 11834.

HOTEL CHOICES

As in many other countries, hotels in Germany are classified by a star rating (from one to five stars). The process of expansion of large hotel chains which began in the early 1980s means that the number of independent hotels has been greatly reduced. If you want to sample a more characteristically German atmosphere go for smaller family-run hotels. Small hotels where the only meal served is breakfast are called *Hotel garni*. You could also stay in a *Pension* or indeed look for the sign *Zimmer frei* (vacancy at a Bed and Breakfast).

10

Useful Words & Phrases

SIGNS TO RECOGNIZE

Ausgang	exit [on foot]
Ausfahrt	exit [for vehicles]
Notausgang	emergency exit
Eingang	entrance [on foot]
Einfahrt	entrance [for vehicles]

kein and **nicht** signal NO

Kein Eingang,	
Kein Zugang	=No entry
Nichtraucher	=Non-smoker
Verboten	Prohibited
Umleitung	Diversion

Polizei	Police
Zoll	Customs
Toiletten	Toilets
Damen/Herren or *D/H*	Ladies/Gentlemen
Besetzt	Engaged
Frei	Free, vacant

WORDS AND PHRASES TO LEARN

Ja	Yes
Nein	No
Bitte (Bitte schön)	Please

[It is also used for 'Don't mention it./It's a pleasure', and by shop assistants with the meaning 'Can I help you?']

Danke
  or *Danke sehr*
    Danke schön
    Vielen Dank
	Thank you

Guten Morgen	Good morning
Guten Tag	Greeting which can be used throughout the day
Guten Abend	Good evening
Gute Nacht	Good night
Auf Wiedersehen	Good bye
Tschüs	'bye
Entschuldigung	

or *Verzeihung*	I am sorry / Excuse me
Wie bitte?	I beg your pardon?
Sprechen Sie Englisch?	Do you speak English?
Ich verstehe (das) nicht	I don't understand
Ist hier frei?	Is this seat free?
Haben Sie Zimmer frei?	Do you have any rooms free
Wo kann ich telefonieren?	Where is a phone I can use

Gibt es hier. . .?
    ein Schwimmbad
    ein Kino
    einen Golfplatz
	Is there a. . .here?
	    swimming pool
	    cinema
	    golf course

Wieviel kostet. . .?	How much is. . .?
Wo ist. . .?	Where is. . .?
Wann. . .?	When. . .?
Hilfe!!	Help!

WORDS AND PHRASES YOU MAY HEAR

Viel Spaß!/Viel Vergnügen!	Have fun! Enjoy yourself!
Gute Reise!/Gute Fahrt!	Bon voyage!
Guten Aufenthalt!	Have a nice stay!
Alles Gute!	All the best!
Frohe Weihnachten!/Frohe Ostern!	Happy Christmas/ Easter!
Vorsicht!/Achtung!	Look out!

Facts About Germany

The Federal Republic of Germany lies at the centre of Europe. It covers an area of 357,000 sq. km, and has a population of 80 million (the largest in the European Union) which also makes it one of the most densely populated countries in Europe.

The capital of Germany is Berlin with a population of 3,472,000. Other major cities include Hamburg (1,706,000), the country's principal seaport and largest centre for overseas trade, Munich (1,250,000), a renowned centre for industry, and Cologne (964,000) famous for fine arts.

German is the native language of more than 100 million people worldwide. As well as in Germany itself, German is spoken in Austria, in a large part of Switzerland, Liechtenstein and in some parts of Luxembourg. There are also German-speaking minorities in Belgium, France, Denmark, northern Italy and in several East-European countries.

Germany is a country of mixed terrain. The north has dry, sandy lowland, heaths and moors, interspersed with many lakes. There are two coastal regions: that bordering the North Sea tends to be marshy, while that bordering the Baltic Sea is more rugged. The Central Upland Range divides the north from the south, with the central Rhine Valley and the Hessian depression providing a natural pathway for north-south traffic arteries. The south-west of this region has a naturally terraced landscape, bearing large areas of forest. To the very south of Germany, the land rises still further into the German Alps.

Zugspitze, in the northern Alps, is Germany's highest mountain at 2962 m.

The distance between the most northern (The Isle of Sylt) and the most southern point (Oberstdorf in the Alps) in Germany is 876 km (544 miles). The longest distance between the easternmost point (Deschka in Saxony) and the westernmost point (Selfkant in North-Rhine-Westphalia) is 640 km (397 miles). The total length of German borders is 3776km (2347 miles).

West Germany (while the country was still divided) was one of the first member states of the EEC (now the European Union) joining in 1958.

Climate

Germany's climate is temperate and sharp changes in temperature are rare. There is precipitation all year round. Average winter temperatures range from 2C in the lowland areas and -6C in the mountains. The Harz Mountains, however, have a climactic zone of their own with cold winds and heavy snow, and even in summer this region is cool. Elsewhere in the summer months (July being the hottest), temperatures are between 18C in low-lying regions and 20C in the sheltered valleys of the south.

About half of Germany's total area is given over to agriculture, while almost a third is covered by forest. There is concentrated vine-growing on the upland slopes of the Rhine valley.

The mainstay of the German economy is industry. Germany is the world's third largest producer of automobiles, and mechanical, electrical and electronic engineering are other major industries. More than 4 million people live in the Rhine-Ruhr industrial agglomeration.

Germany has one of the most efficient national railway systems in Europe, Deutsche Bahn, which links all major towns and cities with a regular and comfortable service. Many rail services link with local bus services. There are concessionary tickets available to non-residents, under the *Euro-*

Domino and Regional Bus Pass scheme, but these must be bought before arrival in Germany. (See Ch.8.)

Road traffic in Germany travels on the right and there is a widespread network of motorways. There are no tolls.

The German currency (to be superseded by the Euro on 1 January 2002) the Deutschmark is equal to 100 Pfennigs. The denominations were 1000DM, 500DM, 200DM, 100DM, 50DM, 20DM, 10DM and 5DM notes and 5DM, 2DM, 1DM, 50 Pfennigs, 10 Pfennigs, 5 Pfennigs, 2 Pfennigs and 1 Pfennigs coins. Credit Cards are widely accepted in Germany and Travellers' Cheques easily cashed.

VAT (consumption tax), currently at 16%, is included in the price of goods and services.

Tipping is voluntary.

Bank opening hours are 8.30a.m.-1.00p.m. and 2p.m.-4.00p.m. Monday to Friday (5.30pm om Thursday). They are closed Saturday and Sunday. Post Offices usually open between 8a.m. and 6.00p.m. Monday to Friday, and between 8a.m. and 12 noon on Saturdays. At stations and airports they may be open longer and sometimes also on Sundays.

There is no state religion in Germany, but at least three-quarters of the population are Christian, almost equally divided between the Roman Catholic and Protestant faiths. There are also small Islamic, Jewish and Orthodox communities. (For more details of these religions please see the companion series *The Simple Guides to World Religions*.)

Education is compulsory in Germany from the age of six. Generally, full-time compulsory education continues for 9 years (10 years in some regions). However, those who leave school after these 9 or 10 years are obliged to attend a vocational school on a part-time basis until they are 18.

Higher education courses in Germany last for a minimum of four years. The average number of years Germans spend at university is six. In some subjects it may take as many as seven to eight years until a student is considered to be qualified. The academic year is organized in semesters.

The Telephone Service

Public telephones are widespread and take coins. Most also accept telephone cards, which may be purchased from Post Offices.

Emergency telephone numbers are Police 110, Fire 112. Medical Assistance numbers vary by location, and may be found either at the site of the telephone or in the local directory.

Germany uses the Metric systems of weights and measures.

Mains voltage in Germany is 220V.

International newspapers and journals are available in most major German cities. Nearly every city also has its own daily newspaper in addition to the large number of national newspapers.

Germans put great emphasis on preserving their cultural heritage. Local authorities are responsible for the upkeep of cultural institutions and the promotion of artistic activities. This means, for example, that theatres do not have to rely on ticket sales for more than about 15% of their income. Thus, even moderate-sized towns and cities have their own theatre companies and orchestras.

German Words Used In This Book

Adventskalender 23	Advent calendar
Auf wiedersehen 32	goodbye
Ausland	overseas
Bahncard 52	Discount railway card
Betreten verboten 30	keep off the grass
Bratwurst 41	fried sausage
Christkind	Christ child
Christkindlesmarkt 23	Christmas market
Das ist OK 43	Fine, OK
Das stimmt so 43	keep the change
Deutsche Bundesbahn 52	German railways
Frau 46	Mrs, wife
Fritten 41	chips (French fries)
Gasthaus	
Gasthof } 43	inn
Glühwein 23	mulled wine
Grillplätz 30	place to barbecue in a public park
Guten Appetit 43	Bon appetit
Guten Tag 32	Hello, good-day
Heilige Dreikönige 24	Epiphany
Herr 46	Mr, man
Kehrwoche	keep-tidy week
Knödel 42	dumplings

Länder	federal states
Lebkuchen	gingerbread
lieblich 42	sweet
Osterhase 26	Easter Bunny
Pros(i)t! 43	Cheers!
Qualitätswein 42	officially tested quality wine
Shulten 28	Large cardboard cone
Sonntagsspaziergang 29	Sunday afternoon work
Stollen	Christmas cake
Suss 42	sweet
Trimm-Dich-Pfade 29	keep-fit trail
trocken 42	dry
Umlaut	two dots above a, o, u
Weihnachtsmann	Father Christmas
Zimmer frei	vacancy (B&B)
Zum Kaffee 40	Invitation to mid-afternoon coffee
Zum Whol 43	good health

Index